THE ASSASSINATION

OF

CHRISTOPHER MARLOWE

MURDER, THOUGH IT HAVE NO TONGUE, WILL SPEAK WITH MOST MIRACULOUS ORGAN.—*Shakspere.*

THE ASSASSINATION

OF

CHRISTOPHER MARLOWE

(A New View)

BY

SAMUEL A. TANNENBAUM

The Shoe String Press, Inc.
Hamden, Connecticut

Offset 1962
from the 1928 edition
Printed in the United States of America

ACKNOWLEDGMENTS

Among the many friends who have patiently or enthusiastically, as the case might be, read my essay on Marlowe's assassination, and who have freely expressed their views on my theory and ungrudgingly argued the subject with me, raising and meeting difficulties, I am especially obliged to PROFESSOR JOSEPH QUINCY ADAMS, MR. MAX I. BAYM, PROFESSOR JOSEPH VINCENT CROWNE, MR. ALEXANDER GREEN, PROFESSOR E. H. C. OLIPHANT, *and* PROFESSOR ASHLEY H. THORNDIKE. *Others to whom I am indebted are the distinguished physicians whose opinions I quote in Appendix A. In common with the rest of the literary world, I am grateful to* PROFESSOR JAMES LESLIE HOTSON, *whose inspiration, intelligence and perseverance brought to light the new documents in the case— the Coroner's report and the Queen's pardon.*

S. A. T.

April 1928.

THE ASSASSINATION OF
CHRISTOPHER MARLOWE

I

The arrest, on May 12, 1593, of Thomas Kyd, the first of the great Elizabethan dramatic poets, on the grave charges of atheism, of meddling in dangerous matters of state, and of publishing seditious libels tending to incite insurrection and rebellion in the English capital, had far more important causes and much more far-reaching consequences than have hitherto been suspected.

Among the causes which led to the inhuman torture on the rack and the untimely death of the popular dramatist, we must reckon—if my reading of the history of the period be right — the idyllic love of one of the most remarkable couples of whom we have any record, the fierce and vindictive resentment of England's greatest queen, as well as the fantastic ambitions and exalted dreams of one of the most gifted and brilliant men of all time.

Among the consequences of the passions thus brought into conflict, we must include the non-completion of the revision of one of the best and most characteristic historical dramas of the period —the tragedy of *Sir Thomas Moore*.[1] This play, undoubtedly written with political intent, was being rushed to completion by no less than six of England's most virile and most versatile poets: the veteran playwright, Anthony Mundy, young Thomas Heywood, fat Henry Chettle, kindly Thomas Dekker, industrious Thomas Kyd, and one—out of all whooping, the best of the group—who has not yet been identified and whom some very able scholars consider to have been none other than Shakspere himself.[2]

But the non-completion of the play was only a trifle in comparison with the

---

[1] *Harl. MS. 7268,* at the British Museum.

[2] That the sixth man, hitherto known as "D", was *not* Shakspere, I have tried to show in my books, *Problems in Shakspere's Penmanship* and *The Booke of Sir Thomas Moore.* The latter of these presents my case for the dating of this play (the spring of 1593) as well as for the identification of Heywood, Chettle, and Kyd.

effects Kyd's arrest had on his career as well as on that of the marvellous Christopher Marlowe, and therefore on the history of English letters. That its completion and performance would have affected the political history of the world in any way may well be doubted.

The more or less immediate circumstances leading to the imprisonment of "sporting Kyd" were these:

Living conditions in London, owing to the increase of population and to unwise legislation, were very hard on the native artisans, mechanics, petty tradesmen, and apprentices. As is usual in such cases, the presence of thrifty and prosperous foreigners was bitterly resented by the natives. This resentment had for several years taken the shape not only of public disturbances and riots, but of admonitions to the unwelcome aliens, mainly refugees from France and Belgium, to get out of the country. Unobserved by the authorities, during the small hours of a night in May 1593, some dissatisfied citizens posted up in various sections of the city placards which warned the foreigners to depart, with bag and baggage, before July 9. One of these posters, only a fragment of which has come down to us, was

found on the wall of the Dutch churchyard. It read:

> *You strangers, that inhabit in this land,*
> *Note this same writing, do it under-*
> *stand;*
> *Conceive it well, for safe-guard of*
> *your lives,*
> *Your goods, your children, and your*
> *dearest wives.*

The Privy Council — in reality, the
National Government — had for more
than a year been protesting against the
outrages perpetrated on the foreign residents and had solicited the Lord Mayor
of the city to apprehend the disturbers
and to seek out and imprison the agita-
tors.[3] Their Lordships went so far as to
instruct the Mayor to have the person
guilty of having written the "libel" ap-
prehended and tortured (though torture
was no part of the English legal system)
if he did not disclose his meaning and
purpose and the identity of his accom-
plices. This was in the early part of
April, 1593. But the Mayor, whose sym-
pathies were evidently with the natives,

---

[3] For additional details regarding the quarrel between
the aliens and the natives, the reader is referred to my
Booke of Sir Thomas Moore.

made no arrests. On April 22, the Privy Council[4] again considered the matter and appointed a special commission "to examine by secret means who maie be authors for the saide [seditious] libelles." Less than two weeks after this, a highly alliterative and bombastic placard was displayed in London in which "the beastly Brutes, the Belgians, or rather Drunken Drones, and faint-hearted Flemings," as well as the "fraudulent Frenchmen" were ordered "to depart out of the Realm of England." Six days later, on May 11, the Council—fearing international complications even more than domestic broils—ordered another commission to use "extraordinary pains" (the equivocal wording may have been intentional) to apprehend the malefactors and to "put them to the Torture in Bridewell and by the extremitie thereof, to be used at such times and as often as you shall think fit, draw [!] them to discover their knowledge concerning the said libells."[5]

The very next day, May 12, 1593, officers of the law entered the study of

---

[4] *The Acts of the Privy Council of England,* 1901, vol. 4, pp. 187, 200, 201, 222.

[5] See *The Booke of Sir Thomas Moore,* pp. 96-98.

Thomas Kyd with a warrant for his arrest
and made a careful search of the premises
for documents of a seditious nature.
Inasmuch as it could not have been the
literary qualities of the posters — verse
tests had not yet been discovered—which
made the authorities suspect Kyd, we are
almost compelled to assume that he had
been betrayed to the Commission by an
informer. That Kyd probably thought
so will appear from what follows.
Whether his arrest was due solely to his
connection, real or supposed, with the
minatory placards, or whether it was also
due to his share in the authorship and
contemplated production of the incen-
diary play of *Sir Thomas Moore,* or
both, it is impossible to say. But the
combination is certainly suggestive.

The search, it is fairly certain, brought
to light nothing of a seditious or politic-
ally objectionable nature. But that did
not save Kyd; his arrest had evidently
been determined on by the Government.
Searching his chamber, the officers discovered something else, something which
furnished them with an excuse for arrest-
ing him and conveying him to Bridewell
prison. This discovery consisted of
three sheets of paper (written in a neat

and easily legible hand) which the officers regarded, or pretended to regard, as a treatise on atheism.[6] The possession of such a document was in those days a dangerous matter, certainly far more dangerous than to have in one's possession literature attacking the French and Dutch residents of the city. The Privy Council frowned on atheism, even though they often dared not prosecute those they suspected to be guilty of the offence.

Fortunately these three sheets of paper have been preserved. The back of the third sheet bears the following inscription, in all probability in the hand of the officer making the arrest: "12 May 1593/ Vile hereticall Conceiptes/ denyinge the deity of Jhesus/ Christe o^r Savior fownd/ emongest the paprs of Thos/Kydd prisoner/."

In connection with this almost lawless arrest three significant facts stand out in bold relief:

---

[6] They were rediscovered by Professor F. S. Boas in 1898 and are preserved in the British Museum, where they bear the mark *MS. Harl. 6848, ff. 187-189.* Professor Boas reprinted them, in reverse order, in his book, *The Works of Thomas Kyd,* London, 1901. His book contains a facsimile of the first page of the alleged treatise. A correct transcript of all three pages and a facsimile of the second page appear in my *Booke of Sir Thomas Moore.*

1. The alleged treatise is, as I have tried to prove in my book on the *Moore* manuscript,[7] in Kyd's handwriting.

2. Kyd, though he must have been aware of the seriousness of the charge against him and of the danger he was in, refrained from entering a general denial in his defence. He could have maintained—correctly, as Professor Boas informs us — that the papers were not atheistical; that they were, in fact, "a defence of Theistic or Unitarian doctrines," and that they were (as Professor W. D. Briggs[8] has recently shown) only a transcript of material contained in John Proctor's book, *The Fall of the Late Arrian* (published in 1549). Instead of making this perfectly obvious plea, Kyd, apparently accepting the officer's characterization of the documents, chose a most remarkable line of defence. He asserted that these papers were not his, that the alleged disputation had, as a matter of fact, emanated from Christopher Marlowe. Thereupon the officer making the arrest added the following words to the

7 *Op. cit.*, pp. 43, 47.

8 "On a document concerning Christopher Marlowe," in *Studies in Philology*, April, 1920, vol. 20, pp. 153-159.

previously quoted notation on the back of
the third page: "wch [papers] he [Kyd]
affirmethe That he/ had ffrom Marlowe."[9]   That these words were added
some time, probably a few days, after
Kyd's arrest, may be inferred from the
following circumstances: the ink   in
which they were written is not that of the
rest of the memorandum (Boas), and the
writing, though in the same hand, is
slightly different (larger and freer).

3 The cautious wording of the alle-
gation regarding Marlowe must be noted.
Kyd was careful not to say that Marlowe
had written the alleged atheistical treatise.   Had he done so, Marlowe would
unquestionably have been able to prove
that the penmanship was not his.   Kyd
did not say that the opinions expressed in
the document were Marlowe's, nor even
that the papers were Marlowe's property.
All he said was that he "had" them from
Marlowe.   From all of which it is fairly
certain that when these memoranda were
written, Marlowe was still alive and that
Kyd thought it best to be cautious in
attacking his former associate.

---

[9] It is not impossible, however, that the endorsement
was the work of a clerk of the Privy Council or of the
prison to which Kyd was committed.

How he came into possession of the dangerous document, Kyd explained subsequently (the date is not known) to the President of the Star Chamber, Sir John Puckering, in a letter in which he pleaded for his Lordship's assistance in recovering his former position in the service of Ferdinando Stanley, Lord Strange,[10] and in which he tried to minimize his relations with the atheist Marlowe. He wrote to his Lordship: "When I was first suspected for that libell that concern'd the state, amongst those waste and idle papers (w.ch I carde not for) & wch vnaskt I did deliuer vp, were founde some fragments of a disputation, toching that opinion [atheism], affirmd by Marlowe to be his, and shufled with some of myne (vnknown to me) by some occasion of o^r wrytinge in one chamber twoe yeares synce."[11]

It will be noticed that, even though Marlowe was dead when this letter was

---

[10] That the Lord whom Thomas Kyd served, probably in the rôle of secretary, was Ferdinando Stanley, I have shown in my *Booke of Sir Thomas Moore,* pp. 38-41.

[11] The whole of this interesting and important letter (*B.M., MS. Harl. 6849, ff. 218-19*) is finely facsimiled (but not accurately transcribed) in Professor Boas' book. The reader will find it in my book, pp. 108-11.

written, Kyd did not say that the alleged atheistical papers were in Marlowe's handwriting. He contented himself with vehemently reiterating his innocence and with alleging that Marlowe, who (he said) made no secret of his atheism, had shared his room with him and that in this way their papers might have got mixed. How long they had shared one chamber he did not say; but it is clear that he was trying to give the impression that it was for only a very short time ("some occasion"), even though that makes it extremely improbable that any of Marlowe's papers should have accidentally got mixed with his without either one having noticed it, and even more improbable that he would not have returned them to his associate or thrown them out.

From Kyd's unnecessarily venomous attack on the character and opinions of "this Marlowe" (as he contemptuously designates him) it seems reasonable to infer that Kyd hated Marlowe and thought that it was he who had betrayed him to the Council. How otherwise, Kyd might have thought, would the authorities have selected his study for such a search, and known what they evidently knew—the very day after the special commission had been appointed. It was impossible for the officers to have pounced on him by chance. Fretting under his supposed betrayal by his quondam room-mate, he wrote to Sir John: "his L[ordshi]p never knewe his [Marlowe's] service, but in writing for his plaiers, ffor never co[u]ld my L[ord] endure his name, or sight, when he had heard of his conditions [*i.e.,* of his atheism], nor wo[u]ld indeed the forme of devyne praiers vsed duelie in his L[ordshi]ps house, haue quadred [— squared] w[i]th such reprobates. That I sho[u]ld loue or be familer frend, w[i]th one so irreligious, were verie rare, when Tullie saith *Digni sunt ami- cita quib[u]s in ipsis inest causa cur diligantur,* w[hi]ch neither was in him, for *p*[er]son, quallities, or honestie, besides he was intem*p*[er]ate & of a cruel hart. . . ."

The inference that Kyd suspected Marlowe to be the author of his woes is further supported by the fact that in a document [12] which was almost certainly written during Kyd's incarceration, and therefore before the letter to Puckering,

12 *B. M., MS. Harl. 6848, f. 154.*

the prisoner declares—in his own handwriting—that it was Marlowe's custom
"in table talk or otherwise to iest at the
deuine scriptures/gybe at praiers, &
stryve in argum[en]t to frustrate & con-
fute what hath byn/spoke or wrytt by
prophets & such holie men/He wold
report S[ain]t John to be o[u]r savior
Christes Alexis.[13] J [= I] cover it with
reverence/and trembling that is that
Christ did loue him w[i]th an extraor-
dinarie [=unnatural] loue."[14]

That Kyd thought he had been betrayed to the Council by an informer is
clearly implied in his attributing his
troubles to an "outcast *Is[h]mael"* who
"for want [*i.e.,* in hope of reward] or of
his own dispose to lewdness [*i.e.,* wicked-
ness] had . . . incensed yo[u]r
L[ordshi]ps [the Council] to suspect
me" (quoted from his letter to Puckering).

---

[13] In Virgil's *2d. Eclogue* Alexis is a beautiful youth
beloved by the shepherd Corydon. This therefore
amounts to a charge of homosexuality.

[14] This important document was discovered by Mr. F.
K. Brown in 1921 and is described in *The Times
Literary Supplement* (London), June 2, 1921, p. 335. It
is finely facsimiled and accurately transcribed in Dr.
W. W. Greg's *Literary Autographs from 1550-1650.* See
also my book, *op. cit.,* pp. 38, 41-44, 52.

But that is not all. The words "outcast *Ismael*" in the above quotation
serve, almost without a doubt, to identify
Kit Marlowe as the informer who betrayed Kyd to their Lordships of the
dreaded Star Chamber. In the epithet
"outcast" Kyd probably meant no more
than that Marlowe's atheism made him a
social outcast, but it is not at all impossible that he had something more specific
in mind. In his letter to Puckering he
says that the patron whom he and Marlowe served could not endure Kit's name
"when he heard of his conditions." In
the one-page memorandum or affidavit
which Mr. Brown discovered, Kyd calls
God to witness that this pious patron had
commanded him, "as in hatred of his
[Marlowe's] life and thoughts," to
break off associations with one who enter-
tained such "monstruous opinions." This
considered, it would not be at all sur-
prising if we should some day discover
that Lord Strange had ordered the troupe
of players bearing his name to sever its
relations with the atheist poet. That the
designation of the informer as an
"Ishmaelite" (a term which the *Standard
Dictionary* defines as "a person whose

hand was against every man") refers to Marlowe's rashness in attempting "soden pryvie iniuries to men"[14a] (Kyd's words) seems almost a certainty.

On May 18, 1593—six days after Kyd's incarceration—the Privy Council issued an order for Marlowe's arrest. It must always remain a matter for great regret that the minutes of the Council, as well as the warrant for Marlowe's apprehension, are silent about the nature of the charges against the younger poet and the identity of his accuser. But, considering the close similarity between the accusations brought against him in the other documents in the case and the offences enumerated in the Kyd memorandum, there can be but little doubt that Marlowe's arrest was due solely to Kyd's charges against him. So certain was Kyd that it was his erstwhile associate who had betrayed him to the authorities that he retaliated by divulging what he knew about him and even by threatening to involve the advanced spirits who permitted Marlowe to share in their freethinking and philosophical debates.

[14a] This probably alludes to the felony with which Marlowe was charged in 1588. (See Professor Hotson's essay, "Marlowe among the Churchwardens," in the *Atlantic Monthly*, July, 1926, vol. 138, pp. 37-44.)

On the 20th day of May Marlowe was under arrest, but not imprisoned. Though at liberty, he was prohibited from leaving the precincts of the city and was "commanded to give his daily attendance to their Lordships [the Council] until he shall be licensed to the contrary." [15] This, it must be granted, was so extraordinary an act of leniency on the part of the Council that, in connection with its knowledge, as the records show, that Kit was to be found at "the house of Mr. T. Walsingham [one of the chiefs of England's secret service] in Kent," we are surely warranted in inferring that the Council did not take the matter too seriously, very probably because it knew that Marlowe was one of the Queen's secret agents, and perhaps, too, that he had been responsible for the arrest of his vindictive accuser.[16]

Just what happened during the first few days after Kyd's arrest can only be

[15] *The Acts of the Privy Council,* May 20, 1593.

[16] That Marlowe was a spy in the service of the Queen and of Sir Francis Walsingham we know from the labors of Professor Hotson (*cf.* the work cited, pp. 63-4) and of Miss Eugenie de Kalb (*cf.* "The Death of Marlowe," in *The Times Literary Supplement,* May 21, 1925, p. 351).

conjectured. From his memorandum to
their Lordships of the Council—which,
in all probability, only repeats what he
had told them orally—we may infer that,
under the stress of "paines and vnde-
served tortures," he had spoken of "men
of quallitie" (members of the nobility)
who kept Marlowe "greater company;"
but, even though he admits that he can
p[ar]ticularize" (=name) some of these,
he carefully refrains from divulging
their identity. He evidently hoped that
some of these men of quality would come
to his rescue.

After Kyd had been given a prelimi-
nary treatment in Bridewells, perhaps with
the "crewel garters" spoken of in Shakspere's *King Lear,* he began to realize
that those who were in peril from him
were not rushing to his rescue. He thereupon ventured a little further and cer-
tified to his torturers that Marlowe "wold
p[er]swade w[i]th men of quallitie"
[still unnamed] "to goe vnto the K[ing]
of Scots whether [= whither] I heare
Royden is gon and where if he [Mar-
lowe] had liv[e]d he told me when I saw
him last he meant to be." This was
clearly intended to inform the Council

and the Queen that some of the foremost men in England were in secret communication with King James of Scotland. To understand the significance of this, we must remember that Queen Elizabeth, ever since the execution of Mary, was in constant fear of what James might do to avenge his mother's cruel death, and that he, on his part, was engaging in a succession of intrigues to secure what, by virtue of his hereditary right and his Protestantism, was virtually already his.[17]

That the Commissioners, or torturers, succeeded in breaking down Kyd's resistance, real or pretended, and "drew" from him the names of some at least of Marlowe's associates, is deducible from his letter to Puckering, wherein he says: "ffor more assurance that I was not of that vile opinion [atheism], Lett it but please yo[u]r L[ordshi]p to enquire of such as he conversed w[i]thall, that is (as I am geven to vnderstand) w[i]th Harriott,[18] Warner,[19] Royden, and some

---

[17] Cf. *The Dictionary of National Biography.*

[18] Thomas Harriott, one of the "three magi" who frequently attended the Earl of Northumberland in the Tower, had acknowledged himself to be a deist. He was a member of Walter Ralegh's group of freethinkers.

stationers in Paules churchyard, whom I
in no sort can accuse nor will excuse by
reason of his companie." Though the
men he names are not the "men of quallitie" he hints at in his memorandum, their
mention enables us to designate the men
he had in mind, ("the men higher up,"
our journalists would say). These men
of quality, who associated with Marlowe
and the three distinguished men just
named, were none other than Sir Walter
Ralegh, Edward Vere [20] (seventeenth
Earl of Oxford), Henry Percy [21] (Earl

---

[19] Walter Warner, the distinguished mathematician,
another one of the Earl of Northumberland's "three
magi," was also one of Ralegh's group. Some think
that Kyd may have meant William Warner, the poet,
the author of the highly praised *Albion's England*.

[20] Edward de Vere, seventeenth Earl of Oxford and
Lord Great Chamberlain, was one of the most talented,
eccentric, extravagant, irresponsible, and intersting men
of the Age of Elizabeth. He was born in 1550 and
died in 1604. He was inordinately quarrelsome, tem-
peramental and reckless, and therewithal endowed with
a high degree of musical talent and literary ability.
Men of letters found him friendly and helpful, and he
was the patron of a company of actors. He was
as erratic in his relations with the Queen as with others,
and in 1592 he fell out with her because she refused to
grant his petition for a monopoly to import into England
certain oils, wool, and fruits—a refusal which doomed
him, for financial reasons, to live in retirement. This
is the man who, in the opinion of some writers, was the
"real Shakespeare."

[21] This was the "wizard Earl," as he was popularly

of Northumberland), Sir George Carey
(afterwards Lord Hunsdon), and
others.[22] These men constituted a not
very popular coterie which a Jesuit
pamphleteer, Father Robert Parsons,
branded as a "school of atheism" in a
book entitled *Responsio ad Elizabethae
Reginae Edictum contra Catholicos*
(published in London in 1592). It is
generally held that the incomparable
Ralegh, at one of whose London houses
these brilliant and daring spirits—scien-
tists, poets and philosophers—held their
weekly discussions, was the leader of the
group, and that for a while his powerful
influence with the Queen protected them
from molestation and perhaps even from
prosecution. Kyd, be it borne in mind,
was not one of this circle.

---

known, whom the Roman Catholics had instigated to
assert and fortify his claim to the English crown and
who fearlessly protested against King James' severity
in his treatment of Ralegh. He was, in all probability,
the first owner of the famous *Northumberland Manuscript.* For an interesting and entertaining account of
this eccentric patron of the arts and sciences, consult the
Dictionary of National Biography.

22 In their edition of *Love's Labour's Lost* (1923, p.
xxxiii), Mr. Dover Wilson and Professor Quiller-
Couch erroneously include the name of the ingenious
Stanley, fifth Earl of Derby, in this group. George
Chapman, the authorities say, was one of the coterie;
Shakspere was not, as far as we know.

The astonishing thing in this whole matter is Kyd's daring to appeal to the testimony of members of Ralegh's unpopular group of freethinkers at a time when Sir Walter himself, never popular either at Court or with the masses, and still in disgrace with the Queen about his liaison and marriage, was by general report condemned for atheism. From certain documents preserved at the British Museum,[23] we know that the Government, alarmed at the spread of atheism, was willing to make a scapegoat of Sir Walter. Not long after the events we have just narrated, Ralegh was, as a matter of fact, under surveillance, and the Court of High Commission ordered him, his brother, and some of their intimate friends, to be examined (at Cerne, in Dorsetshire) on March 1, 1594. "The examinations," says Mr. Boas,[24] "do not seem to have been followed by any proceedings against Ralegh, but the discovery [which he made during the hear-

---

[23] An account of these documents (*MS. Harl. 6842, ff. 183-90*) and extracts from them were published by Mr. J. M. Stone ("Atheism under Elizabeth and James I." in *The Month* for June, 1894, vol. 81, pp. 174-87) and by Professor Boas (in *Literature*, Nos. 147 and 148).

[24] *Works of Thomas Kyd*, p. lxxiii.

ings] that even his private table-talk was not safe from espionage may well have helped to hasten him forth on his adventurous quest for an El Dorado across the southern main." It is worth noting that during the examinations Harriott[25] was several times referred to and that once he was spoken of as an "attendant" on Sir Walter Ralegh.

Kyd was by no means the only one to accuse Marlowe. On Whitsun Eve, May 29, 1593, the Privy Council received a "Note"[26] from one Richard Baines[27] (not "Bames"), charging Marlowe, the associate of cutpurses and masterless men, with the foulest blasphemies. In this document, in the informer's own hand, Baines

---

[25] Harriott was again coupled with Marlowe in a letter (*Harl. MS. 6848, f. 176*) written to Justice Young by a spy concerning Cholmely and his "crues." We may recall that at Sir Walter's trial, in 1603, Lord Chief Justice Coke branded the accused as "a damnable atheist" and denounced him for associating with that "devil" Harriott.

[26] This "note Containing the opinion of on[e] Christopher Marly, Concerning his damnable Judgment of Religion and scorn of gods words" (*Harl. MS. 6848, fol. 185-6,* also *Harl. MS. 6853, fo. 320*) has been reprinted in an expurgated version by Boas (*op. cit.,* pp. cxiv-cxvi), by Ingram (*op. cit.,* pp. 260-2) and in Mr. H. Ellis's "unexpurgated" edition of Marlowe's *Plays* in the *Mermaid Series* (1893, pp. 428-30). It is transcribed, without abridgement, in my *Notes and Additions to 'The Booke of Sir Thomas Moore.'*

accuses Marlowe of maintaining that
Harriott, the brilliant scientist and in-
ventor, whom the fool multitude regarded as a magician, and whom he de-
scribes as "Sir W. Raleighs man," could
"do more" than Moses who "was but a
Jugler." He goes on to aver that "on[e]
Ric[hard] Cholmley hath Confessed
that he was perswaded by Marloes Reasons to become an *Atheist.*" The seriousness of this charge will be realized when
it is noted that this Cholmelie (or Cham-
ley) was known to have organized a company of "atheists" as well as to have enter-
tained revolutionary political designs,
and that Baines[27] further charged Marlowe with having claimed "as good a
Right to Coine as the Queen of England."

How Marlowe would have met these
grave charges, each punishable by death,
must remain a matter of conjecture. He
was not destined to reply to them, however, for on the very next day, May 30,

---

[27] Concerning Baines we are told by Mr. Havelock
Ellis (*op. cit.,* p. xliv) that he "was hanged at Tyburn
next year for some degrading offence," but, as Mr. Ellis
says, "there seems no reason—while making judicious·
reservations—to doubt the substantial accuracy of his
statements."

this "famous gracer of tragedians" was assassinated by Ingram Frizer, "gentleman," a notorious rascal and a proved habitual swindler. The only witnesses to the homicide were one Nicholas Skeres and one Robert Poley, the former a cheat and jailbird who had been associated with Frizer in some of his nefarious schemes, and the latter a spy.[28] Here, it will be acknowledged, was an excellent trio for a contrived murder. I say "contrived murder" because, from Mr. Hotson's account of the matter, it is clearly apparent that the story told at the Coroner's inquest by Skeres and Poley (the only witnesses to the assassination) is incredible.[29] The circumstances considered, it seems to me much more likely that on that fatal Wednesday, Marlowe was lured [30] to Eleanor Bull's inn at Deptford Strand, was wined liberally till he fell into a drunken stupor; the

[28] That Poley was a "secret agent" we know from Conyers Read's *Mr. Secretary Walsingham*, 1925, II. 383. For additional information about him, see Mr. Chambers' review of Hotson's book, in *Modern Language Review*, 1926, vol. 21, pp. 84-85.

[29] For a translation of the Coroner's report, see pp. 71-75.

[30] William Vaughan, who has given us (in his *Golden Grove*, 1600) the most nearly authentic account of the assassination, tells us that Ingram invited Marlowe to

time being ripe and Eleanor Bull safely out of the way in another part of the building, Ingram Frizer deliberately plunged his dagger into Marlowe's brain to a sufficient depth to cause his instant death.

The assumption that Marlowe's death, contrary to the Coroner's report (*q.v.*), was premeditated assassination, not accidental homicide in self defence, is warranted by the following considerations.

1. The two wounds on Frizer's head were too slight to have been inflicted by a man in a rage wielding a sharp dagger. In this connection we must not overlook the significance of the fact that no physician seems to have been called in to dress Frizer's wounds, which were probably too slight to require medical attention. That each of the two wounds on Frizer's head was two inches long and a quarter of an inch deep is so curious a phenomenon as to warrant the assumption that they were self-inflicted. A dagger thrust from above downward or from below upward

_____

Deptford "to a feast." Neither Frizer, Skeres, nor Poley, be it remembered, gave the Coroner any explanation of how they happened to meet Marlowe that morning and why they did not leave him out of their sight all day.

is much more likely to make a punctured wound of variable depth than an incised wound two inches long and only a quarter of an inch deep. (Parenthetically it may be noted that the number "two" seems to have been a favorite with the Coroner in this case.)

2. The only witnesses to the fatal fray were two disreputable friends of the man charged with the killing.

3. Frizer and his friends kept Marlowe company in the tavern, or the grounds adjoining it, from about ten o'clock in the forenoon until night. None of these men explained to the Coroner's jury how he happened to be idle that day and disposed to loaf at Eleanor Bull's tavern all those hours. There is nothing in the evidence to show they had ever been there before or even that they knew the place. And it certainly is strange that both Poley and Skeres (who, as far as the Coroner's evidence shows, may not have been acquainted with Marlowe) should have expected Marlowe to pay for their suppers.

4. It is incredible that Marlowe should have been lying on a cot and that Frizer should have had his back toward

him while they were engaged in an acrimonious discussion.

5. The Coroner's statement that Frizer, while sitting in a chair and wrestling with a man in bed behind him, inflicted "a mortal wound over his [assailant's] right eye of the depth of two inches & of the width of one inch" is so improbable as to throw doubt on the whole of his account of the matter.

6. Neither Skeres nor Poley made the slightest attempt to interfere with or to part the combatants. There is no indication that they attempted to summon help.

7. The Coroner apparently made no attempt to find any other persons who ate or drank at Eleanor Bull's that day and who might have testified to the behavior of this remarkable quartet. How was it that none of the habitués of the place, a cheap tavern frequented mainly by sailors, were called upon to say what they knew or saw? The Coroner's strange silence suggests that Frizer, Skeres, and Poley probably managed to keep Marlowe most of the day in a private room and out of view of any of Eleanor's patrons. We must not overlook the sig-

nificance of the fact that the Coroner reports that Marlowe and his associates "met together in a room in the house . . . & there passed the time together & dined" and that, after walking about in the garden belonging to the house, they "returned . . . to the room aforesaid & there together and in company supped."

8. The Coroner's failure to get Eleanor Bull's tetimony is a highly suspicious feature, especially in view of the fact that the law required him to question the neighbors and any other persons who might throw any light on the homicide. It would surely have been of the utmost importance to know whether there were any evidences of a struggle, *e.g.,* overturned chairs, broken dishes, the position of Marlowe's body, etc. As matters stand, we do not even know for certain whether the dead Marlowe was discovered in bed or on the floor, whether there were bloodstains in the bed, whether the Coroner found the dagger in the wound and in the clutch of the deceased—surely very material facts in an inquiry regarding a possible murder. And yet Eleanor Bull did not testify. The only likely explanation for this fact is that the assassin

or assassins kept Marlowe in a private room in a remote part of the house until they were ready to dispatch him. Having got him sufficiently drunk, one of them thrust a dagger into the sleeping Marlowe's brain just above his right eye.

9. That the Coroner's inquest was a perfunctory matter and that his story cannot be accepted as a faithful account of what actually transpired is sufficiently evident from the facts that he made no inquiry into how much liquor Marlowe had imbibed and that he was willing to believe that a two-inch wound above the eye would result in instant death. One who knows the anatomy and pathology of the human brain knows that it is almost impossible for death to follow immediately upon the infliction of such a wound.[31] That Marlowe's brain—"the abode of the poet's vaulting imagination," as Hotson poetically calls it—was not examined is, therefore, certain, and yet the Coroner says that the wound was two inches deep and one inch wide. Such a wound, if made horizontally, traversing the eye socket, would not have involved

---

[31] For expert medical opinions on this matter, see pp. 65-67.

the brain for more than half an inch, and would not have affected any vital area; if the wound was made vertically, the injury would have been in the frontal lobe of the brain and would not have proved fatal, certainly not immediately. To have caused instant death the assassin would have had to thrust his dagger horizontally into Marlowe's brain to a depth of six or seven inches—and that could not have happened if Frizer and Marlowe had been wrestling as the witnesses described. Portions of the frontal lobe have been shot away without fatal consequences. Bullets have been known to enter the brain through one temple and to come out through the other without causing death. The Coroner's "grim tale" of Marlowe's violent and untimely end is, therefore, not a true account of what happened.

* * * *

Taking all the known facts into consideration, we must, it seems to me, conclude (1) that Marlowe was assassinated while he was asleep, probably in a drunken stupor; (2) that while he was in this condition, Ingram Frizer thrust his twelve-penny dagger, which he had brought with him for the purpose, deeply into Marlowe's brain; and (3) that the Coroner was influenced by certain powers not to inquire - too curiously into the violent death of an "outcast *Ismael*".[32]

---

[32] It is at least interesting to note that the day before Marlowe's cruel end Richard Baines had included in his report to the Privy Council these words: "I think all men in Cristianity ought to indevor that the mouth of so dangerous a member [as this Marlowe] may be stopped." Was this a mere coincidence? or was it a broad hint to their Lordships of what was about to happen? or was it only an unintended betrayal of a secret of which the writer had cognizance? That it was not the pious indignation of a good Christian which prompted Baines' prophetic utterance is sufficiently evident from what we know of that worthy's career.

II

If, then, Christopher Marlowe did not make his "great reckoning in a little room" accidentally but was the victim of a deliberate and planned murder, it seems impossible not to believe that the outrage was the outcome of the events immediately preceding it and intimately connected with Kyd's difficulties and accusations. To accept this view we need only think that Kyd, living in a city having a population of over one hundred thousand, was pounced upon by the police on the very day following the Privy Council's action; that Kyd could not but suspect that Marlowe, his quondam roommate, had betrayed him to the officers of the law; that in his defence he attributed the incriminating "disputation" to Marlowe; that he subsequently charged Marlowe with numerous criminal offences (atheism, Socinianism, blasphemy, converting others to atheism, plotting against the State); that, not content with this, he named certain men— Harriott, Warner, Royden—with having associated with the "outcast *Ismael*" and listened to his atheistical doctrines; and that he very clearly threatened to divulge the identity of certain "men of quallitie" who (he implied) were not only intimates of the "outcast" but were leagued with him in conspiring with King James against Queen Elizabeth. At the same time we must not lose sight of this significant fact—Marlowe was the subject of attack from other quarters too. Baines' report to the Council not only duplicated and confirmed Kyd's charges, but added the grave accusations that Marlowe openly advocated sexual perversions, claimed to have as good a right to coin as the Queen of England had, and had converted at least one other to atheism. In another spy's memorandum (*MS. Harl. 6848, fo. 190*) "Sr Walter Raliegh & others" are coupled with "one Marlowe [who] is able to shewe more sounde reasons for Atheisme then any devine in Englande is able to geue to prove devinitie." That Marlowe, one of Walsingham's secret agents, was being apprised of the powerful forces at work to destroy him can hardly be doubted. He must have realized now that his ex-associate

knew too much, suspected him, and was
ready to sacrifice everything and every-
body to save himself and to be revenged
on the causer of his miseries. Kyd was
safe in jail and was being closely guarded
by the authorities, who hoped that the
names of the "men of quallitie" he had
implicated might yet be "drawn" from
the prisoner.

And what about the "men of quallitie"
whose lives were being threatened?
From what we know of the characters of
the Council's spies we may safely assume
that these noblemen were not wholly
ignorant of what Kyd had charged them
with and what certain spies had reported
to the Council. There were "leaks" in
those days, as there are now. That Marlowe's situation was desperate is certain.
The only ones who could have saved him
—by the use of their political influence—
were the men who were most in danger
from him. From Kyd's reticence—a
politic reticence, no doubt—the "men of
quallitie" knew that they were safe if he
was. Marlowe was the only one they
had cause to fear. Marlowe, therefore,
had to be silenced.[33] Ingram Frizer, a

---

[33] That such dastardly plotting was not beyond an

servant of Mr. Thomas Walsingham, and therefore an associate of Marlowe (and not likely to be distrusted), was assigned the task of stopping the poet-spy's career. Nicholas Skeres and Robert Poley were schooled to corroborate the assassin's defense. Kyd was instructed to hold his tongue and wait. May 30th came and Marlowe walked into the trap which had been set for him. What followed we know.

When we attempt to answer the question what Englishman or Englishmen of that day could have been so situated as to be in sufficiently great danger from Marlowe's possible revelations to desire his death, it seems that we must restrict our investigation to the "men of quallitie" who constituted Sir Walter Ralegh's coterie. And when we consider that Sir Walter was not only hinted at in Kyd's accusing memorandum but was actually named in Baines' "Note," that he had a reputation for atheism, and that a few

---

Elizabethan nobleman is clearly shown by the statement in the *Dictionary of National Biography* that the Earl of Oxford, Edward de Vere, "was said to have deliberately planned the murder of an antagonist, and he very reluctantly abandoned what he affected to regard as a safe scheme of assassination."

months later he had to submit to being examined regarding his religious views, we have no choice but to focus our attention on him. When, in addition to the facts just mentioned, we find him so constituted as to be eminently capable of so bold and ruthless an act as the assassination of an enemy in the furtherance of his own interests, and so situated as to be almost driven to such an act of desperation, it becomes a reasonable assumption that the responsibility for Marlowe's violent and cruel taking-off should be laid at his door.

Tradition says that Marlowe was one of the choice spirits who were received at the weekly gatherings of brilliant literary and scientific men at Sir Walter's house, "where religious topics were often discussed with perilous freedom." Mr. Ingram, following Dyce, says (*Christopher Marlowe and his Associates,* 1904, p. 184): "The earliest references to the poet not only allude to his friendship with Raleigh but even assert that he read a paper on the Trinity before Sir Walter Raleigh and his brother Carew and others at the Knight's house." [34] The alleged

---

[34] In the spy's affidavit Cholmeley is reported as say-

friendship is in all probability a myth, though Ralegh must have been fascinated by the creator of Tamburlaine and Faust, two portraits in which that bold and aspiring spirit may very well have seen himself. But the relations between them were probably of a sufficiently intimate nature to cause Sir Walter considerable anxiety on learning—as he must have learned—that this "god of undaunted verse," who had enjoyed his hospitality, was not only a disciple of Machiavelli but a secret agent of the Government and had been responsible for Kyd's arrest. That at this critical moment Marlowe might have made it clear to Sir Walter that he looked to him to save him is not at all improbable. But Ralegh knew that he was then in no position to do what was demanded of him.

To an ambitious, cruel, and unscrupulous Elizabethan adventurer, to such a "soldier, sailor, and courtier" as Ralegh was—careers which he himself subse-

---

ing that Marlowe had told him that "he hath read the Atheist lecture to Sr Walter Raleigh & others." For Marlowe's relations with his contemporaries the reader should consult Professor Tucker Brooke's essay, "Marlowe's Reputation," in *Trans. of the Conn. Acad. of Arts & Sciences,* 1922, vol. 25, pp. 347-408.

quently blamed for his "courses of wickedness and vice" (his own words)—the removal by assassination of a dangerous foe, who might not only frustrate the fulfilment of his dreams but land him in the Tower, or worse (especially at a time when he was in disgrace with the furious Elizabeth and the subject of almost universal hatred and obloquy), was as obvious as it was practicable. This many-gifted, brilliant, enigmatical Englishman —as striking a case of dual personality as history affords—was capable of "unspeakable cold-blooded cruelty," of "treachery and false faith," of "bold unscrupulousness," of almost "any act of baseness." That is the verdict of those of his biographers (Stebbing, Gosse, Buchan, Thoreau) who are not obviously his apologists. Ralegh's wanton brutality and wholesale butcheries in Ireland— "that commonwealth of common woe," as he called it—is one of the saddest and darkest pages in the history of the English-Irish troubles. To attain his ends all means were permissible. Is it any wonder, then, that "he was hated by all and sundry, from the citizens of London to the courtiers who jostled him in the

Queen's antechamber"? [35] To the popular mind, and even to the best men of his
day, "Raleigh remained the ambitious
courtier, the able and unscrupulous soldier, and the man who wrought ever for
his own ends." To this vain, egotistical
man, this victim of an insatiable passion
for fame, wealth, and rule, who dreamed
of founding empires, and who realized
all too keenly how his many enemies—
envying him for his great wealth, his os-
tentation, his adventures, his talents, his
special privileges—would revel in his
ruin,—to such a man it would have been
the most trivial undertaking to sweep out
of his path a hot-headed, quarrelsome,
vainglorious, and treacherous son of a
shoemaker, a fellow whom he had be-
friended and admitted into the privacy
of his sanctum. He knew, none so well
as he, that his and his friends' fortunes
were desperate. if Marlowe divulged
what he knew.

To understand what Ralegh's state of
mind was at this time it is necessary to
recount the occurrences of the preceding
year. After having for several years
played the rôle of devoted and impas-

[35] J. Buchan, *Sir Walter Raleigh,* pp. 41. 45.

sioned lover to the Virgin Queen—
"love's queen and the goddess of his life"
—he had permitted himself to fall a victim to the charms of one of the Queen's
maids of honor, the witty, beautiful (tall,
slender, blue-eyed, golden-haired) and
altogether lovely Elizabeth Throgmor-
ton, some thirty-five years younger than
her royal rival. The Queen, "who loved
the presence of handsome young men
with unmaidenly ardour," notwithstanding her alleged prudery and the sixty
years she carried on her ulcerous back,
was furious—"fiercely incensed," says a
contemporary.[35]   Sir Walter was immediately dismissed from the royal favor
and committed to the Tower where he
was detained from June to September,
1592. While imprisoned there, he be-
haved like a spoiled child, quarrelling
with his keepers, bemoaning his hard lot,
and writing lovesick letters to the Queen
—even though his betrothed was con-
fined in a suite only a few feet from his.
    During his confinement in the Tower he
discovered another grievance against his
"Belphoebe:" she prohibited him from
sharing to the full in the expedition of
1592 which ended in the capture of the

great Spanish carack, the "Madre de Dios." And, besides, the Queen's greed made the division of the spoils so extremely unequal that he, "to whom the success was owing, who bore the toils and burden of it all, was considerably the loser," whereas Lord Cumberland (who had invested only a relatively small sum in the piratical venture) made £17,000 profit.

Circumstances into which we need not now enter brought about his release from the Tower. But "freedom from confinement did not bring with it a return of the royal graciousness, and for some years he was practically an exile from the Court" (Buchan). Early in 1593 he was in retirement at his manor of Sherborne in Dorset, where he spent the time in hunting, hawking, cultivating potatoes, and attempting to grow tobacco. That this sort of life, coupled with ostracism from the Court (the latter extended also to his wife), must have been dreadfully galling to this bold and adventurous spirit, always hankering for battle and enterprise, can hardly be doubted. He seems to have been firmly convinced that in his case the Queen—who had been

known to overlook the fickleness of lovers
—would be obdurate and never again
have anything to do with him. Here,
then, at the age of forty, he saw his career
ended, his dreams of power and rule
shattered.

Would he permit himself to be doomed
to a life of inaction and obscurity, to
"keep a farm and carters?" Of course
he would not. We know that he brooded
on schemes of maritime adventure as an
escape from the boredom to which an
insulted Queen had banished him. London fascinated him and drew him like a
magnet; the records show that he paid
frequent visits to the capital. To keep in
touch with the world he had himself
elected to Parliament—and to his credit
be it said that, notwithstanding the odium
in which he was generally held, he took
a lively interest in public affairs and
championed what was just and reasonable in popular demands.

The Queen took advantage of every
means in her power to harass him and
make him feel the settled hate in her
heart. Thus, she now made him recall
all his people from Ireland where he had
established a colony on his estates in the

Counties of Westford and Cork; after Michaelmas, 1594, she ordered him to pay a rental of 100 Marks (instead of the 50 Marks he had been in the habit of paying) for one of his Irish estates. (See Malone's *Variorum*, 1821, vol. 2, p. 573.)

That he was watching his opportunity to get back into power, to find an outlet for his talents, to get into the limelight in the political arena, rather than to be restored to the Queen's good graces, seems to be proved by several circumstances. He protested loudly — no doubt more loudly than the circumstances warranted —against the Government's blundering policies as regards Ireland, and advocated a resolute and consistent despotism, sustained, if necessary, by treachery and murder. About this time—on February 28, 1593, to be exact—he also advocated open war with Spain. Three weeks later he opposed the bill in the House of Commons for the extension of the privileges of aliens in England. In the discussion of the latter measure he was the only one who spoke of expelling the strangers.

Sir Walter's attitude to the foreigners who were the objects of the city's "exceeding pitiful and great exclamations" at this time is deserving of careful attention. So grave was the situation that it occupied the House of Commons during several sessions (March 21, 23, and 24, 1593). Unmindful of the humanitarian pleas of some of his associates (Mr. Finch, Sir Robert Cecil, and others), Ralegh expostulated: "Whereas it is pretended, That for strangers it is against Charity, against Honour, against Profit to expel them; in my opinion it is no matter of Charity to relieve them. . . . I see no reason that so much respect should be given unto them. And to conclude, in the whole cause I see no matter of Honour, no matter of Charity, no Profit in relieving them." [36]

That his policies on public questions were the expression of his secret purposes cannot be doubted. A man, constituted as he was, conscious of his powers, his talents, his unemployed energy, his versatility, his military ability and skill, his scientific attainments, his popularity with the crews of his ships,[37] his ambitions,

---

[36] Cf. *A Compleat Journal of the Notes, Speeches and Debates, both of the House of Lords and House of Commons throughout the whole Reign of Queen Elizabeth.* Collected by . . . Sir Simonds D'Ewes, London, 1693, pp. 504-9.

and smarting under the disabilities attendant on being in disgrace, would without a doubt be keenly on the alert for any opportunity that chance might offer to bring him back into a position of influence and power.

Sir Walter, like others of his distinguished contemporaries, was capable of treasonous intrigue against his Queen. This may reasonably be deduced from a letter of his written—on July 6, 1597—to the none too scrupulous Robert Cecil. In that letter he says: "I acquaynted the L: Generall [*i.e.,* The Earl of Essex] wth your . . . kynd acceptance of your enterteynment; hee was also wonderfull merry att ye consait of Richard the 2. I hope it shall never alter, & whereof I shall be most gladd of, as the treu way to all our good, qu[i]ett, & advacemet, & most of all for her sake whose affaires

---

37 When the Queen released Ralegh from the Tower to go to Dartmouth to settle the disputes about the distribution of the spoils taken on the "Madre de Dios," Robert Cecil wrote home: "I assure you, Sir, his poor servants to the number of one hundred and forty goodly men, and all the mariners, came to him with such shouts and joy, as I never saw a man more troubled to quell in my life; for he is very extreme pensive longer than he is busied, in which he can toil terribly."

shall therby fy[n]d better progression."
This passage has been a hopeless conun-
drum to the biographers, but as Edward
Edwards has shown,[38] there can be little
doubt that it refers to Shakspere's *Richard the Second* which was then being
performed at the Globe Theatre. It will
be recalled that this tragedy, destined to
play an important rôle in 1601 in the
treasonous enterprise of the Lord General Essex, at this time included the cele-
brated "deposition scene" (IV. i, 154-
318) which the Queen, conceiving that
Richard II was a mask for herself,
sternly disapproved of.[39] To the psy-
chologist there will be profound significance in the unusual (and hitherto un-
noticed) subscription to the above letter
by Ralegh: "Sir, I will ever be yours:
it is all I can saye, & I will performe it.
with my life & wth my fortune." He
wrote better than he knew.

But let us return to 1593. Being in the
frame of mind we have already described, and knowing that he could rely

---

[38] *The Life of Sir Walter Ralegh*, 1868, vol. 2, pp.
164-9.

[39] *Cf.* S. Lee, *A Life of William Shakespeare*, 1916,
pp. 129, 254-5.

on the crews of his ships and the men of
Devon, this malcontent must have
thought of ways and means of bringing
about some situation which would enable
him to play a conspicuous part, get close
to the Queen, oust his enemies from the
Court, and possibly even take charge of
the Government, as Essex planned to do a
few years later. His life at the Court
had acquainted him with the arts of in-
direct dealing. The hostility between
the natives and the aliens and between the
city and the national Government seemed
to offer the coveted opportunity. We
must remember that at this time he was
in London a great deal; that he advocated
publicly the expulsion of the aliens; that
he was attempting to fan into a flame the
smouldering anti-Hispanism, was openly
criticising the Government's Irish policy,
and was not without powerful political
friends.[40]

40 That he had friends in the Privy Council seems
to be indicated by the following interesting circum-
stance: in the official replica (*Harl. MS. 6853, fo. 320*),
laid before Queen Elizabeth, of Richard Baines' note
accusing Marlowe of blasphemy, the designation of
Harriott as "Sir W Raleighs man" was omitted- surely
not for the purpose of sparing the Queen's feelings.
And nine months later the Commission, which had been
appointed to examine him at Cerne, apparently squashed
the matter after it had heard all the witnesses and ob-

It seems not too far-fetched, therefore,
to conjecture that directly or indirectly,
possibly with the assistance of his intimate associate, his other self, Harriott,[41]
he convinced the manager of a theatrical
company, preferably the Admiral's, that
a play dealing with Sir Thomas More
and the "ill May day" of 1517 would be
timely and might prove a money maker.[42]
Munday, "our best plotter," and his
young associates, Heywood and Chettle,
were entrusted with the task. They at
once betook themselves to Hall's *Chron-
icle,* familiarized themselves with More's
career, met together to outline the play,

'tained sufficient evidence to convict him, his brother
and Harriott, had it wished to do so.

[41] Harriott, and therefore Ralegh, was mentioned not
only in every one of the documents we have referred
to in connection with the charges of heresy and blasphemy but also in connection with plots against the
Government.

[42] That *Sir Thomas Moore* was written for a political purpose was clearly felt by Professor Ashley
H. Thorndike; in 1916 (*Shakespeare's Theater, p. 213*),
when we knew a great deal less about this play than
we now know, he expressed surprise that Tyllney
"should have permitted in any form a play intended
to excite feeling against the foreigners dwelling in
London." That the drama was 'universally used for
political purposes' in Shakspere's time is convincingly
shown in Richard Simpson's paper, "The Political Use
of the Stage in Shakspere's Time," in *The Transac-
tions of the New Shakspere Society,* 1874, part II, pp.
371-95.

[42] That Sir Walter, like some of his intimate asso-

and set to work. Fortunately or unfor-
tunately, however, for the course of history, the writing and revision of the play
did not go on to completion. The plague,
which drove the actors out of London,
may have had something to do with it,
but the greater likelihood is that the re-
visers were interrupted by the informer's
betrayal of Kyd's participation in a plot
to expel French and Flemish subjects
from London. And thus the plan center-
ing around the tragedy of *Sir Thomas
Moore* came to naught. For the time
being, Sir Walter Ralegh's plots to be
revenged on an unreasonable and irasci-
ble queen were frustrated, but, unfortu-
nately for English literature, not before
Christopher Marlowe had become so
enmeshed in them that they cost him his
life.

---

ciates, *e.g.*, Edward de Vere, had intimate contacts with
theatrical companies, is fairly certain. On January 30,
1597, Rowland Whyte wrote to Sir Robert Sydney as
follows: "My Lord Compton, Sir Walter Rawley, my
Lord Southampton doe severally feast Mr. Secretary
before he depart, and have Plaies and Banquets."
(*Letters and Memorials of State,* ed. by Arthur Collins,
1746, vol. 2, p. 86.)

III

Appendix A

OPINIONS OF
MEDICAL EXPERTS

III

Dr. Charles A. Elsberg, of New York City, distinguished consulting neurological surgeon, wrote me on March 19, 1928, as follows:

You are quite right in the assumption that it would be very unusual for a "dagger wound just above the right eye, two inches deep and one inch wide," to have caused instant death, altho it is possible that if Marlowe had a very thin skull and short frontal region that the dagger might have penetrated the cavernous sinus. This seems to me, however, very improbable. On the other hand, if Marlowe was suffering from a cardiac disease, a sudden shock might have caused instant death, altho it was not the actual trauma.

* * *

Dr. James Ewing, professor of pathology at Cornell University Medical College (New York City), sent me the following reply to my letter to him regarding Marlowe's death:

I do not see how the wound that you describe by a dagger entering the orbit above the right eye could cause instant death. Yet it seems possible that if the dagger went deeply into the brain, it might sever blood vessels and cause hemorrhage which would lead to almost immediate unconsciousness and death in a short time, without recovering consciousness.

* * *

Professor W. G. MacCallum, head of the department of pathology at Johns Hopkins University, wrote me as follows:

I should think that a wound such as you described . . . would hardly have gone further than through the frontal sinus and into the frontal lobe of the cerebrum and I don't see either how it caused instant death.

Of course, one might imagine that the force of the blow was such as to stun him and allow time for fatal haemorrhage in that position. The only other thing one could think of would be perhaps that with extreme violence some further injury might have been produced in a more vital part of the brain, but on the whole it seems to me questionable that instant death would follow such a blow.

* * *

Dr. Otto H. Schultze, professor of pathology and medical jurisprudence, Coroner's physician in New York from 1896 to 1914, medical assistant District Attorney of New York County from 1914 to date, and the author of several works on the medico-legal aspects of homicide, wrote as follows in reply to my inquiry:

A stab wound of the skin or even puncturing the orbit could not cause instant death, nor would be likely to cause a fatal hemorrhage. A stab wound above the eye, penetrating the orbital plate and frontal lobe of brain, may cause death, but hardly would account for "instant" death.

IV

APPENDIX B

THE CORONER'S REPORT

IV

Kent./ Inquisition indented taken at
Detford Strand in the aforesaid County
of Kent within the verge on the first day
of June in the year of the reign of
Elizabeth by the grace of God of England France & Ireland Queen defender
of the faith &c thirty-fifth, in the presence
of William Danby, Gentleman, Coroner
of the household of our said lady the
Queen, upon view of the body of Christopher Morley, there lying dead & slain,
upon oath of Nicholas Draper, Gentleman, Wolstan Randall, gentleman, William Curry, Adrian Walker, John Bar-
ber, Robert Baldwyn, Giles ffeld, George
Halfepenny, Henry Awger, James Batt,
Henry Bendyn, Thomas Batt senior, John
Baldwyn, Alexander Burrage, Edmund
Goodcheepe, & Henry Dabyns, Who say
[upon] their oath that when a certain
Ingram ffrysar, late of London, Gentleman, and the aforesaid Christopher Morley and one Nicholas Skeres, late of
London, Gentleman, and Robert Poley of

London aforesaid, Gentleman, on the thirtieth day of May in the thirty-fifth year above named, at Detford Strand aforesaid in the said County of Kent within the verge, about the tenth hour before noon of the same day, met together in a room in the house of a certain Eleanor Bull, widow; & there passed the time together & dined & after dinner were in quiet sort together there & walked in the garden belonging to the said house until the sixth hour after noon of the same day & then returned from the said garden to the room aforesaid & there together and in company supped; & after supper the said Ingram & Christopher Morley were in speech & uttered one to the other divers malicious words for the reason that they could not be at one nor agree about the payment of the sum of pence, that is, *le recknynge,* there; & the said Christopher Morley then lying upon a bed in the room where they supped, & moved with anger against the said Ingram ffrysar upon the words as aforesaid spoken between them, And the said Ingram then & there sitting in the room aforesaid with his back towards the bed where the said Christopher Morley was then lying, sitting near the bed, that is, *nere the bed,* & with the front part of his body towards the table & the aforesaid Nicholas Skeres & Robert Poley sitting on either side of the said Ingram in such a manner that the same Ingram ffrysar in no wise could take flight: it so befell that the said Christopher Morley on a sudden & of his malice towards the said Ingram aforethought, then & there maliciously drew the dagger of the said Ingram which was at his back, and with the same dagger the said Christopher Morley then & there maliciously gave the aforesaid Ingram two wounds on his head of the length of two inches & of the depth of a quarter of an inch; whereupon the said Ingram, in fear of being slain, & sitting in the manner aforesaid between the said Nicholas Skeres & Robert Poley so that he could not in any wise get away, in his own defence & for the saving of his life, then & there struggled with the said Christopher Morley to get back from him his dagger aforesaid; in which affray the same Ingram could not get away from the said Christopher Morley; and so it befell in that affray that the said Ingram, in defence of his life, with the dagger afore-

said of the value of 12d. gave the said
Christopher then & there a mortal wound
over his right eye of the depth of two
inches & of the width of one inch; of
which mortal wound the aforesaid Christopher Morley then & there instantly
died; And so the Jurors aforesaid say
upon their oath that the said Ingram
killed & slew Christopher Morley aforesaid on the thirtieth day of May in the
thirty-fifth year named above at Detford
Strand aforesaid within the verge in the
room aforesaid within the verge in the
manner and form aforesaid in the defence
and saving of his own life, against the
peace of our said lady the Queen, her now
crown & dignity; And further the said
Jurors say upon their oath that the said
Ingram after the slaying aforesaid perpetrated & done by him in the manner &
form aforesaid neither fled nor withdrew
himself; But what goods or chattels,
lands or tenements the said Ingram had
at the time of the slaying aforesaid, done
& perpetrated by him in the manner and
form aforesaid, the said Jurors are
totally ignorant. In witness of which
thing the said Coroner as well as the
Jurors aforesaid to this Inquisition have

interchangeably set their seals.
Given the day & year above named &c
                    by William Danby
                              Coroner.*

---
* For permission to reprint this English version of the
Coroner's report I am indebted to Professor Hotson.